LIKE A VIRGIN

WITHDRAWN

Gordon Steel

LIKE A VIRGIN

OBERON BOOKS
LONDON

First published in 2000 by Oberon Books Ltd
521 Caledonian Road, London N7 9RH
Tel: 020 7607 3637 / Fax: 020 7607 3629
e-mail: oberon.books@btconnect.com
www.oberonbooks.com

Reprinted 2005

A catalogue record for this book is available from the British
Library.

ISBN: 1 84002 140 3

Cover illustration: Andrzej Klimowski

Cover typography: Jeff Willis

Printed in Great Britain by Antony Rowe Ltd, Chippenham

*Lyrics for songs written by Gordon Steel except for 'Sisters of
Sin', lyrics by Mark Benton. Music by Mark Benton. A cassette is
available upon request from Alan Brodie Representation.

For Glenda, Rebecca, Jack and Hannah

Characters

ANGELA
16 years old

VIV
her mother, in her early thirties

KEN
her father, in his late thirties

MAXINE
her best friend, also 16 years old

MONKEY
an aspiring musician, 24 years old

Like A Virgin was first performed by the Hull Truck Theatre
Company at the Dovecot Arts Centre, Stockton-on-Tees on 15
August 1995 with the following cast:

ANGELA, Caroline Wardle
VIV, Carole Copeland
KEN, Michael Hodgson
MAXINE, Samantha Seager
MONKEY, Michael Hodgson

Director, Gordon Steel

The cast for the national tour was as follows:

ANGELA, Jill Halfpenny
VIV, Carole Copeland
KEN, John Tierney
MAXINE, Vicky Entwhistle
MONKEY, John Tierney

Director, Gordon Steel

ACT ONE

Prologue

ANGELA is alone on stage. She is waiting. Music starts. Her attitude changes and she starts to sing.

ANGELA:

WE DICED WITH DANGER OUT ON THE STREET
WE KISSED THE MOMENT AND PLAYED IN THE HEAT
KNICKING OFF SCHOOL
BREAKING THE RULES

DOWN BY THE RIVER WITH A COUPLE OF CIDERS
WE HAD THE RHYTHM WITH MADONNA INSIDE US
KNICKING OFF SCHOOL
BREAKING THE RULES

ROCKING AND ROLLING, SWEARING AND SMOKING
A FEW DIAMOND WHITES, WE WERE LAUGHING AND JOKING
NOTHING COULD SCARE US, NOTHING DETER US
THE MOMENT WAS OURS AND THE BOYS HAD TO SHARE US

SHOPPING AT MARK ONE, TRYING TO LOSE WEIGHT
SQUEEZING OUR BODIES INTO A SIZE EIGHT
KNICKING OFF SCHOOL
A COUPLE OF FOOLS WHOAH

FLIRTY AND FIFTEEN, WE HAD ALL THE MEANS
STRUTTING AND POSING AND REIGNING SUPREME
KNICKING OFF SCHOOL
BREAKING THE RULES

ROCKING AND ROLLING, SWEARING AND SMOKING
A FEW DIAMOND WHITES, WE WERE LAUGHING AND JOKING
NOTHING COULD SCARE US, NOTHING DETER US
THE MOMENT WAS OURS AND THE BOYS HAD TO SHARE US...
                                        SHARE US...SHARE US...

The Leyton living room. As ANGELA finishes singing KEN bursts into the room pursued by VIV. The scene takes place in ANGELA's head. ANGELA observes and participates in the scene.

KEN: There's no point in making a scene, I'm going and that's that.

VIV: Oh that's it you're going. You're just walking out the door and what am I supposed to do? Carry your friggin' case.

KEN: I've tried to explain.

VIV: That's not an explanation.

KEN: What do you want me to say?

VIV: What do I want you to say! I want you to say that you're not going.

KEN: Viv, for Christ's sake it's not working. I can't go on like this. *We* can't go on like this. If I go now we'll both have a chance.

VIV: Oh I've heard the lot now. By going you're doing me a favour. That's awfully good of you, you big-hearted bastard.

KEN: Do you have to swear?

VIV: Yes I fucking do. You are leaving me and our...*your* child. *Your* daughter. What sort of a life will your daughter have without her dad?

KEN: For Christ's sake, that's enough.

VIV: No, it's not enough. You're a slut. You're walking out on your family to shack up with some young tart.

KEN: (*Slaps her.*) That's enough, Viv...that's enough...

VIV: You've never hit me before. Ken...Kenneth what have I done that is so wrong? One more chance, Ken. I'll be a good wife. I won't want much. (*She goes down on her knees.*) I'm begging you Ken don't leave me. Please… Please.

KEN: Viv, what the hell are you doing? For God's sake don't…don't…keep your dignity…bloody hell.

VIV: Keep your dignity. Christ! Why? Why? Is that because that's all I've got left? I've looked after you like a friggin' saint. I even gave you…you're the only man I've ever…I've ever…What a joke.

KEN: I'm going 'cos this is getting us nowhere.

VIV: That's your answer for everything isn't it. Walk away, you coward. Go on, piss off.

ANGELA: Mam!

KEN and VIV shocked, turn and talk to an imaginary eight-year-old, ANGELA.

KEN: Go to bed, darling. Come here, I'll carry you up.

VIV: Daddy's leaving us, angel. Daddy doesn't love you anymore. Daddy doesn't love you.

KEN: Christ Viv, what the hell are you saying.

VIV: Daddy is going away.

KEN: Viv, stop it!

VIV: He is going to live with another woman.

KEN: She's only eight years old.

VIV: And he is going to have another family. Another little girl to take your place because he doesn't love you any more.

KEN: What the hell are you saying? What are you trying to do to her?

ANGELA screams. There is a long silence. KEN quickly turns, picks up a suitcase and his guitar case and goes to exit. ANGELA speaks. KEN stops in the doorway.

ANGELA: Daddy, Daddy, please don't leave me. I'll be good. I'll tidy my room up and I promise I won't make a noise when you're watching the telly or reading the paper. (*Pause.*) I'll give you peace. I'll try honest. I promise.

There is a silence. KEN and ANGELA stare at each other. KEN can bear it no longer and leaves quickly. VIV walks to the door, closes it and exits through the up-stage door. ANGELA is alone on stage.

He's not coming back, Oscar. Viv says that he doesn't love us any more…but I know that can't be right. We've prayed, haven't we Oscar. Is it me, Oscar? Am I horrible? Was it my fault? He said he loved me. He said he'd always love me.

Loud music jolts ANGELA from her thoughts. We are in the toilets of a nightclub. ANGELA resumes her waiting.

Scene 1

The toilets of the Madison nightclub. ANGELA holds a bottle of Diamond White which she drinks through a straw.

ANGELA: Maxine, what are you doin'?

MAXINE: I'm shakin' me lettuce.

ANGELA: Aw come out Maxine, you've been in there ages.

MAXINE: So.

ANGELA: It bloody stinks in here. Are you havin' a shit?

MAXINE: Don't be so bloody simple, you know I never have a shit when I'm out.

ANGELA: What?

MAXINE: You know what I mean. I can't shit anywhere unless I'm in our house.

ANGELA: Well what the hell 'ave you been doing in there all this time? Making your will?

MAXINE: (*Bursting into tears.*) It's him. It's that bastard Jamie Power. 'E's gone off with Shirley Windows. He had three dances with me. I even bought him a drink.

ANGELA: Aw come on, Maxine. Look, there's no one in here now. Oway, sort yourself out in the mirror before anybody comes in.

MAXINE: Are you sure there's nobody there?

ANGELA: No, hurry up.

MAXINE: Right. (*She appears with face covered in tear-stained mascara.*)

ANGELA: Come on Maxine don't go upsetting yourself. Not over Jamie Powers.

MAXINE: But I love him.

ANGELA: You don't. You know you don't.

MAXINE: I do. I do. I love everything about him. I love his mam. I love his Escort and the scar going down his left cheek. I just love him. What's he doin' with that little tart when he could have me? I'm gorgeous. Why did he do it to me?

ANGELA: He's a twat. 'Ave nowt to do with him.

MAXINE: But I love him.

ANGELA: Yeah I know you do, but if you really want to get him you have to ignore him.

MAXINE: But I love him.

ANGELA: Treat him mean, keep him keen.

MAXINE: He's sexy. Look at the state of me face.

ANGELA: There's nowt I can do about that.

MAXINE: Me make-up you cheeky cow. Look at it, it's exploded. Bloody hell.

ANGELA: Right Maxy baby. We are gonna go out and take this place by storm.

MAXINE: We are?

ANGELA: We certainly are. We'll show that turd what he's missing. Who the hell is Shirley Windows? She's a right doyle.

MAXINE: Yeah you're right. I'm too good for him.

ANGELA: Course you are.

MAXINE: I'll make him squirm.

ANGELA: Course you will.

MAXINE: Who does he think he is?

ANGELA: He's a nobody. He's about as exciting as… as…'Going for Gold'. It's his loss.

MAXINE: I'll show him exactly what he's not going to have.

ANGELA: Are you ready?

MAXINE: You bet your vacant personality I am.

ANGELA: Well, let's go.

They perform an elaborate dance routine and then explode out of the toilet.

Scene 2

The living room of the Leyton House. VIV is sat on the settee. It is late afternoon. ANGELA enters.

ANGELA: What are you doing?

VIV: I've got a headache. Just a couple of paracetamols.

ANGELA: Viv, you know what the doctor said.

VIV: It's my nerves. For God's sake, don't start moralising.

ANGELA: Viv, I'm worried about you. You're gonna kill yourself, you know that.

VIV: I just need to steady my nerves down a bit. It's been a bad week.

ANGELA: And so was last week and the week before that. Do you want rid of me? Is that why you're doing it?

VIV: It's not easy for me you know. I've got bills up to me eyeballs and now bloody Sister Theresa's telling me to lay off my medication.

ANGELA: It's killing you.

VIV: It is prescribed by the doctor because of my condition.

ANGELA: You can't go on like this, Viv, you're gonna have to fight it. You're gonna have to try. It's no good laid there feeling sorry for yourself. The world doesn't owe you a living.

VIV: Have you finished?

ANGELA: I'm just worried about you, you're becoming a joke.

VIV: Oh it's easy for you to say, isn't it? It's easy to point the friggin' finger. What am I supposed to do? Come on, what am I supposed to do?

ANGELA: Try!

VIV: Try. You don't know the meaning of the word. You don't know what it feels like to be…to be. If he'd a died it would have been easier. I could have handled that. People don't die on purpose.

ANGELA: Perhaps if you could get a job you'd feel better.

VIV: Don't be so bloody naïve. How the hell can I earn a decent living? You meet more people in the dole office, than in the pub. They should 'ave a riot round here. They should, they should 'ave a riot. And I'll tell you why, 'cos then somebody might do something. Do you think I'm fat? Do you think my bum's too big? Does it stick out? Do you think people find me attractive? (*Silence.*) I caught these workmen looking at me the other day. They were, they were looking at me. I got a wolf whistle. Me! He was gorgeous, he was blonde and he didn't have his shirt on. He had a lovely bronze tanned body. I caught him looking at me. You can tell can't you. You know when someone's attracted to you. It's physical. It's chemistry. He'll probably ask me out. I can see it coming. Why am I so ugly? Why does nobody like me, love me? (*She screams, cries and sobs.*)

ANGELA: Come on, Viv. Sssh. Sssh. You've got me. You'll always have me. By hell, Viv, you can be melodramatic. You should be on the stage making speeches like that.

Music – Madonna singing 'Vogue'. Lights change.

Scene 3

ANGELA's bedroom. As the lights come up the girls are singing along to 'Vogue'.

MAXINE/ANGELA: Vogue, Vogue.

MAXINE: I've got a secret.

ANGELA: Hey, look at this. (*She dances energetically.*)

MAXINE: You look nowt like her.

ANGELA: Oway then tell us for God's sake.

MAXINE: God I'm gorgeous.

ANGELA: You'll be gorgeous and dead if you don't hurry up and tell us.

MAXINE: Angela my sweet, this big hunk of sexiness has managed to get us a gig.

ANGELA: What?

MAXINE: Yeah.

ANGELA: You mean…

MAXINE: Yes I do.

ANGELA: You're jokin' me.

MAXINE: Cross me heart. We're on. I've done it. In four weeks time we're on. I've managed to get us a gig.

The girls scream. MAXINE leaps on to ANGELA and they dance around singing 'one-nil to the mighty Reds'.

ANGELA: Where?

MAXINE: Grangetown British Legion. Vogue, Vogue.

ANGELA: (*Stunned.*) Grangetown! 'Ang on. (*ANGELA turns off the cassette.*) Is this some kind of joke?

MAXINE: Would I lie to you?

ANGELA: Well you usually do.

MAXINE: Angela!

ANGELA: Oh yeah what was it last week when I was off school, what did you tell them?

MAXINE: Eh? I can't remember.

ANGELA: Well I can. You told them I'd gone to the clinic for an AIDS test. Bloody embarrassing.

MAXINE: Angela, I have sorted us out a gig. Honest. Swear on your life.

ANGELA: Honestly.

MAXINE: Honestly.

ANGELA: Swear down.

MAXINE: Swear on me dad's life. We have got a gig.

ANGELA: I'm gonna wet meself.

MAXINE: They had a cancellation and he said that he wanted a young band like ours to fill the slot.

ANGELA: I'm definitely gonna wet meself.

MAXINE: It was my natural charm that sold the day.

ANGELA: What else?

MAXINE: As soon as he saw me that was it.

ANGELA: Did he say owt else?

MAXINE: I think he fancied me. Understandable I suppose.

ANGELA: For Christ's sake did he say owt else?

MAXINE: I didn't talk to him for very long. He had a bad case of B.O. and shit teeth. He only had four and they all pointed in different directions.

ANGELA: 'Ang on, you said band.

MAXINE: What?

ANGELA: You said band.

MAXINE: (*Innocently.*) Did I?

ANGELA: We haven't got a band.

MAXINE: Do you think my hair's getting too long?

ANGELA: This is bloody brilliant.

MAXINE: I might get it cut if I can cadge some money off our dad.

ANGELA: We'll never work again.

MAXINE: We've never worked before so that'll be no hardship.

ANGELA: What've you done that for?

MAXINE: Calm down for Christ's sake, it's only Grangetown British Legion, not Wembley Stadium. And I told him that we'd performed a couple of times before an' all.

ANGELA: Oh I don't believe you.

MAXINE: He didn't want a new band. What was it he said, 'New bands are always shite-full of young kids wanting to be famous.'

ANGELA: Where have we performed before?

MAXINE: I can't remember. I did say that we'd never performed round here so no one'll ever know.

ANGELA: So let me get this straight. We are performing in Grangetown British Legion with a band we haven't got, singing songs that we haven't got. Bloody brilliant.

MAXINE: Take a chill pill. We'll get one. There'll be hundreds of people dying to perform with me.

ANGELA: There's one over here who's dying to perform on you.

MAXINE: Hey we could become Madonna lookalikes.

ANGELA: Madonna's not that much of a tart.

MAXINE: I'm sure I've got the body for stardom.

ANGELA: Grangetown British Legion. Have you ever been there? You need a prison sentence to get in. People have performed there and they've never been seen again. They've just disappeared. How we gonna get there? I'm not walking through Grangetown without a tattoo. I'm gonna top meself. I'm definitely gonna do meself in.

MAXINE: Look, I think we'd better do what we came round here to do.

ANGELA: I feel sick. Grangetown British Legion. I'm too young to die.

MAXINE: Once they clap eyes on me they'll melt.

ANGELA: They'll melt anything in Grangetown if they can get a couple of quid for it.

MAXINE: Do you think I'd suit me hair up?

ANGELA: But if we're writing songs we've got to be original.

MAXINE: But I can do a great Madonna. She's like me. She's got sex appeal.

ANGELA: That's the problem.

MAXINE: What, that you haven't got any?

ANGELA: Grow up. Madonna was great a few years ago but we've got to move on. Go with the times.

MAXINE: Madonna's brilliant, ask most of the world 'cos they've got her friggin' records.

ANGELA: I know, but we've got to appreciate her for what she is. Love Heart.

MAXINE: You like her. 'May I hope'.

ANGELA: 'Fanciable'. We've got to say more in our music.

MAXINE: So we can become a Number One hit.

ANGELA: Exactly.

MAXINE: Oh like (*She sings to the tune of the chorus from Whigfield's 'Saturday Night'.*) Da da da dum dee dee bollocks bollocks shite.

ANGELA: Funny.

MAXINE: Well, get a life. Hey how about… (*She sings to the tune of 'No Limits', but sings 'No lyrics' instead.*)

ANGELA: Alright clever shit, all I'm saying is…

MAXINE: Keep your hair on, I know what you're saying and I've already started.

ANGELA: You what?

MAXINE: That's shocked you hasn't it. I 'ave, I've started.

ANGELA: What?

MAXINE: I wrote some lyrics last night when I was sat on the loo.

ANGELA: Well, come on then.

MAXINE: Have you started?

ANGELA: No.

MAXINE: Huh.

ANGELA: Look, yes donkey-snot, it's great that you've started, now get on with it. Come on then.

MAXINE: Alright. Well you know at school the other day and senile Simpson was going on about when Margaret Thatcher was in Middlesbrough walking round the derelict areas.

ANGELA: So.

MAXINE: Well I've written a song about it.

ANGELA: You haven't.

MAXINE: Yeah. Just a few lines you know, as you do…
when you're a songwriter.

ANGELA: Let's hear them then.

MAXINE: Right. (*Goes to her bag and takes out a scruffy piece
of paper. She clears her throat.*) I don't think you'll like
them.

ANGELA: Maxine, for crying out loud, get on with it.

MAXINE: Right. (*Sees clears her throat again and composes
herself, before catching sight of herself in the mirror.*) God,
you're gorgeous.

ANGELA: Maxine!

MAXINE: Here goes. I haven't got a tune but I thought we
could work one out later.

ANGELA: Am I gonna hear them or not?

MAXINE: Right.

'I went down town to see Margaret Thatcher
I wanted to get my hands on her but I couldn't catch her
There's no work round here everyone's on the dole
She just does nothing I wish she'd shut her arsehole'

Pause.

What do you think?

ANGELA: It's pathetic.

MAXINE: You what.

ANGELA: Oh come on, you're not serious! 'I wanted to get
my hands on her but I couldn't catch her.'

MAXINE: It rhymes!

ANGELA: Yeah but it may have escaped your notice but there's more to it than that.

MAXINE: Owee then where's yours? Naaaa. At least I've done sommat.

ANGELA: Yeah I bet Madonna's shitting herself.

VIV: (*Off.*) Angela are you up there?

ANGELA: Shit, it's Viv.

The girls frantically start tidying up the bedroom, desperately wafting away the cigarette smoke.

Lights and music.

Scene 4

The Leyton living room. ANGELA is sitting reading magazines. Madonna booms out from a ghetto blaster. The room is a mess. VIV enters.

VIV: Why aren't you at school? (*She starts to take off her coat.*)

ANGELA: Eh? Oh I've been to the doctor's. Anyway, I'm naffing sick of it.

VIV: I've told you about that kind of language.

ANGELA: Oh yeah and you've got a mouth like a flower.

VIV: I'll lamp you if you talk to me like that. Look at the state of this coat, it's bloody pitted. What have you been to the doctor's for? (*She takes a tablet and starts tidying up.*)

ANGELA: It's 'cos I'm tired. I think I'm run down. I went for a tonic.

VIV: Tonic! I'll give you a tonic but you won't like it. Tonic! Anyway you can't not go to school.

ANGELA: It's boring.

VIV: A tonic! (*She switches off the tape.*)

ANGELA: They don't teach yer owt.

VIV: You need an education.

ANGELA: What for?

VIV: You won't get a job without one.

ANGELA: You won't get a job with one.

VIV: You've got an answer for everything. You always have to have the last word.

ANGELA: What good are the names of Henry the Eighth's wives to me?

VIV: You've got to go to school.

ANGELA: He was a mucky bastard anyway.

VIV: I'm warning you. You're just bloody bone idle. A tonic!

ANGELA: And what was it the other day, specific gravity. How will that help me, eh? Come on, how will a knowledge of that help me to get a job?

VIV: You'd fall off the bloody planet without it, you silly sod.

ANGELA: Give me strength.

VIV: Mind you, I think you're already there. Your bloody head's in the clouds.

ANGELA: 'Ere we go.

VIV: Madonna this. Madonna that.

ANGELA: I wondered how long it would be.

Pause.

VIV: Anyway listen, I wanna tell you something. Listen, I've got a job.

ANGELA: Yeah an' you've stopped drinking an' all.

VIV: I have, I've got myself a little part-time job.

ANGELA: What are you doing, wine-tasting?

VIV: Why don't you take me seriously for once?

ANGELA: Owee then hit me with it.

VIV: Cleaning.

ANGELA: Cleaning!

VIV: Cleaning.

ANGELA: The only thing you ever cleaned out was Threshers.

VIV: A house! I'm cleaning somebody's house.

ANGELA: Well they obviously haven't been round here.

VIV: Look it's a job isn't it. I'm trying. I've managed to get myself a little job.

ANGELA: I'm sorry, Viv. Course I'm pleased. Will you do us a favour though?

VIV: What?

ANGELA: Keep it. Don't blow it. Hang on to it.

Silence.

VIV: Course I will. This is it. This is me. The new me on the road to recovery.

ANGELA: Make sure you look smart. I'll clean your shoes.

VIV: I'll wear me Levis. Smart but casual, ready for work.

ANGELA: And when you've finished make sure you wash out your cloths.

VIV: You what?

ANGELA: That's what they told us at school if you ever get a cleaning job: make sure when you've finished you wash your cloths and hang them out to dry.

VIV: What a good idea, that'll create the right impression. What would I do without you?

ANGELA: Just make sure that you're there in plenty of time.

VIV: I'm not stupid. Anyway I don't have to go far, it's only in Shelley Crescent.

ANGELA: Hey, that's not far, brilliant.

VIV: I know, it couldn't have worked out better. Cleaning! It looks as though it doesn't need cleaning. It's only a couple of hours a week but you know what I'm looking forward to most of all?

ANGELA: What?

VIV: Having a reason for getting up in the morning. I wouldn't care, it's a lovely house. I think he's an accountant. It's at the Sigsworths.

ANGELA: The Sigsworths.

VIV: Yeah.

ANGELA: Margaret Sigsworth's.

VIV: Yeah it's a lovely house.

ANGELA: She's in my class at school.

VIV: I know.

ANGELA: You can't work there.

VIV: Why not?

ANGELA: Why not. Why not. You know perfectly well why not. That toffee-nosed little bitch is in my class.

VIV: Oh come on Angela, grow up.

ANGELA: No, you come on.

VIV: It's a job. It's only a little part-time job, but it's a job.

ANGELA: You don't understand, do you? I get enough stick at school about the situation we're in. About…you. The taunts.

VIV: You'd better watch what you're saying.

ANGELA: The little bitchy comments that are said in jest that I have to smile about and pretend they're not bothering me.

VIV: I don't understand. I've got a job. I've actually got a job. Do you know what that means? Do you?

ANGELA: How can I go to school now?

VIV: Will you stop thinking of yourself and think of somebody else for a change?

ANGELA: Listen to you. All I ever get is you. You, you, you. 'Am I too fat?' 'I'm not very well.' 'I got whistled at today.' Since when have you ever given me a thought.

VIV: I've given you everything I've had.

ANGELA: Yeah, trouble, insecurity, neglect, embarrassment. Thanks a bundle.

VIV: You selfish, lying, ungrateful little bugger.

ANGELA: Me? What about you? Every time you're in trouble you blame the pills or the drink. Where do I fit into your life? I'm just the remains of a bad memory. Someone who's been in the way when you wanted to go out and couldn't find a babysitter. God, the houses I've slept in. The strangers that's looked after me. I'm just someone who's around to remind you of your failed marriage. (*She runs out.*)

VIV: Where are you going? You get back here. You get back in this house. Do you hear me?

Lights and music.

Scene 5

ANGELA's bedroom. ANGELA is lying on the bed writing. MAXINE enters hurriedly. ANGELA leaps off the bed and switches off the ghetto blaster which has been playing Madonna songs.

ANGELA: Have you brought the newspaper?

MAXINE: Keep your hair on. I've bought one.

ANGELA: What've you bought one for, there's always loads in your house?

MAXINE: Yeah but you know what our dad's like. He sits on the *Daily Express* while he's reading the *Daily Mirror*. He has to read 'em first. (*She hands ANGELA a cassette.*)

ANGELA: I've been looking for that.

MAXINE: There's hell in our house if you get the paper before he does. Anyway I thought we'd be better off with a posh one.

ANGELA: Bloody hell, *The Times.*

MAXINE: Why can't we just write a love song?

ANGELA: 'Cos everyone writes love songs.

MAXINE: Well, what's wrong with that? Have you seen Jamie Power lately? He's full frontal.

ANGELA: Phugh!

MAXINE: What does that mean?

ANGELA: Oh come on Maxine, he's a right poser.

MAXINE: He's rampant. And if he's very lucky he just might get this beautiful body. No, he's just cool and sophisticated…like a Chippendale.

ANGELA: The only time he ever smiles is when he's passing wind.

MAXINE: He's a hunk.

ANGELA: He's not a patch on Gary Towers.

MAXINE: Eh!

ANGELA: He's not.

MAXINE: I knew you fancied him.

ANGELA: Eh!

MAXINE: Gary Towers.

ANGELA: Maxine, I don't fancy him.

MAXINE: Gary Towers eh. Well, well, well.

ANGELA: Maxine, I do not fancy him. I just think he's better looking and a nicer person than Jamie Power, that's all.

MAXINE: Sure you do.

ANGELA: Maxine!

MAXINE: I won't tell more than a dozen people.

ANGELA: Will you stop twisting everything I say?

MAXINE: Well, you're talking shite.

ANGELA: He is.

MAXINE: Gary Towers, do me a favour. He'd shag the crack of dawn if it had hairs round it.

ANGELA: That's disgusting.

MAXINE: Well he's not worth taking your knickers off for.

ANGELA: Look, let's just get on with it. Hey, there's a riot in Chicago: four dead and 33 injured.

MAXINE: That's a stag night in Middlesbrough.

ANGELA: Maxine, are you gonna take this seriously?

MAXINE: I wanna write songs about love and sex.

ANGELA: We've been through all this. We're gonna say something in our lyrics. Hey, what about this: 'Romanian babies brought to this country'.

MAXINE: Well, that's bloody stupid.

ANGELA: What is?

MAXINE: Bringing little Romanian babies to this country and then dumping them with an English family.

ANGELA: What are you on about?

MAXINE: Well it's obvious thicko. They'll speak a different language, won't they?

ANGELA: (*Pause.*) I worry about you. I don't know why we're bothering even trying. What are we doing this for?

MAXINE: Well I know why I'm doing it.

ANGELA: I daren't ask.

MAXINE: 'Cos I want to be famous.

ANGELA: Everybody wants to be famous.

MAXINE: You know how I'll know when I've really made it? You know what I want most of all?

ANGELA: A dirty weekend with Jamie Power.

MAXINE: No, that's second. I wanna be on 'This is Your Life'. I've dreamed of being on 'This is Your Life' with all these famous people comin' on. That'd be brilliant.

ANGELA: Well if we are gonna make it we've got to be different and not like every other club band. We need a gimmick.

MAXINE: I'd love to see me nana's face when she comes round that screen. 'Eeee our Maxy love haven't you grown – I'm so proud of you.' That'd be brilliant.

ANGELA: Maxy.

MAXINE: What?

ANGELA: I wanna ask you a favour.

MAXINE: What is it?

ANGELA: I want you to lend us some money.

MAXINE: Give over, I've got nowt.

ANGELA: Yes you have, you liar. You said you had loads in the Building Society.

MAXINE: That's for me holidays.

ANGELA: I'll give you it back.

MAXINE: It's for me holidays.

ANGELA: You've just said that. I'll give you it back. (*Long pause.*) Have you lost weight?

MAXINE: Yeah I have, two pounds, can you tell? NO!

ANGELA: You look dead skinny.

MAXINE: You can fuck off.

ANGELA: Oway Max. You wouldn't 'ave snogged Jamie Power last week if I hadn't of paid you in Madison.

MAXINE: No.

ANGELA: And I got your drinks in all night. Oway Max. Please Maxy.

MAXINE: How much?

ANGELA: (*Mumbling.*) Fifty pounds.

MAXINE: What?

ANGELA: (*Shouting.*) Fifty pounds!

MAXINE: Fifty pounds! It's me holiday money.

ANGELA: Look I think we've established the fact that it is your holiday money. Look, I'll give you it back. I promise. I will pay you back. Brownies honour.

ANGELA leaps on top of MAXINE who is sitting on the bed and tickles and manhandles her, grabbing her boobs. MAXINE laughs and struggles free.

MAXINE: Gerrooff you lezzer. (*Pause.*) Bloody hell, what do you want if for?

ANGELA: Well, it's private. I'd rather not say.

MAXINE: PRIVATE! It's my piggin' money and you'd rather not say. You can naff off.

ANGELA: Max. Max, we're the best of friends. You know you can trust me. It's only £50, it's not all of it. Come on Max.

Pause.

MAXINE: Well, you'd better pay me back or you'll be taking a very long walk off a very short pier.

ANGELA: (*Smiling.*) Thanks.

MAXINE: Bye bye Salou. How am I gonna get to Salou if she gets all me holiday money. Shit, I forgot.

She takes a copy of 'More' magazine out of her bag and holds it up for ANGELA to see. ANGELA, excited, goes to pinch it.

ANGELA: Let's have a look then.

They sit on the bed.

MAXINE: Here it is: 'Position of the Fortnight.' (*She looks astounded.*) Look at that.

ANGELA: My God.

ANGELA/MAXINE: Bloody hell.

ANGELA: That's why they don't 'ave position of the week.

MAXINE: Why?

ANGELA: It'll take us two weeks to work the bloody thing out. What's the difficulty rating?

MAXINE: Five. Bloody hell that's the most difficult.

ANGELA: Well I'm not trying it out then.

MAXINE: Why not?

ANGELA: 'Cos the last time the difficulty rating was five you farted in my face.

MAXINE: I didn't.

ANGELA: Yes you did and don't you deny it.

MAXINE: Would I lie to you?

ANGELA: You can't lie straight in bed.

MAXINE: Alright, but I didn't do it on purpose.

ANGELA: No.

MAXINE: I didn't. I couldn't help it. It was that curry our dad made. You know what his curries are like.

ANGELA: Well it didn't exactly slip out, did it? You nearly put the windows through…and it was right in my face. It stunk.

MAXINE: I won't fart, I promise.

ANGELA: You'd better not.

MAXINE: Come on, we always try the positions out just in case. You never know you know when this position might come in handy.

ANGELA: Oway then but this time I'm the woman.

MAXINE: You were the woman last time.

ANGELA: I was not.

MAXINE: You were 'cos I had that banana stuck in me trousers and I had to lift you up and I nearly put me back out.

ANGELA: Well you'd better not fart.

MAXINE: Don't be stupid. Come on.

ANGELA: What does it say?

MAXINE: 'GETTING IT RIGHT.'

ANGELA: Haven't they got, 'getting it at all'?

MAXINE: Do you want me to read this or not?

ANGELA: Sorry.

MAXINE: 'Your partner lies flat on his back. Then you climb on top of him.'

ANGELA: Woah the Hokey Cokey. Woah the Hokey Cokey.

The girls dance around singing 'The Hokey Cokey'.

MAXINE: Go on then, lay down.

ANGELA jumps on the bed and lays down.

You put your big thing in, your big thing out…

ANGELA/MAXINE: In out, in out, you shake it all about.

MAXINE clumsily clambers on top of ANGELA.

MAXINE: Okay darling I'm coming down.

ANGELA: Be careful you silly get or I'll never have a sex life.

MAXINE grabs hold of ANGELA's boobs.

MAXINE: Look at these big buggers.

They laugh.

Angela, you've got a bogey right up your nose.

MAXINE kisses ANGELA on the lips.

ANGELA: Gerroff you kinky cow.

They are both laughing and being stupid.

What next?

MAXINE: Shit I've left the book down there. 'Ang on.

MAXINE retrieves the book.

ANGELA: Your bloody brains are in your tits.

MAXINE: Shut it. I've got it, 'aven't I. Right. 'Then you climb on top of him facing away from him.'

ANGELA: You what!

MAXINE: That's what it says: '…You climb on top of him facing away from him.' How the friggin' hell do I do that?

ANGELA: Just turn over. But be careful for God sake, me boobs are tender.

MAXINE: Graeme Finchley?

ANGELA: Shut it.

MAXINE: Right, here goes.

ANGELA: Bloody hell, you baby hippo, what've you been eating?

MAXINE: Shut it, I've lost two pounds.

She performs the movement with some difficulty. Once in position ANGELA reaches up and grabs MAXINE's boobs.

MAXINE: Gerroff you kinky bitch.

ANGELA: You fat slug.

MAXINE: Shut it. Right, listen. 'Gently lower yourself on to his erect penis.'

They shriek with laughter.

Are you ready?

ANGELA: As I'll ever be.

MAXINE: Coming down.

MAXINE lifts herself up and then bangs down on to ANGELA who screams out.

ANGELA: Aaaaarrrgghh! You've snapped it off, you've snapped the bloody thing off.

MAXINE starts banging up and down rhythmically and the girls continue to shriek.

Ride 'em, big boy.

MAXINE: Eeeeh ah!

ANGELA: It feels good.

MAXINE: Is the earth moving for you?

ANGELA: I think me bowels are.

MAXINE: (*Screaming and groaning.*) Jamie. Jamie and his Magic Torch.

As they continue VIV enters and stands shocked, confused and disbelieving. Eventually the girls notice her and clamber up trying to control their sniggers.

VIV: What are you doing?

ANGELA: Nowt.

MAXINE: (*Hardly able to speak.*) Yeah.

There is an uncomfortable pause as the girls try to control themselves.

VIV: There's somebody at the door for you.

She exits and the girls collapse into laughter.

MAXINE: Oh shit it's my surprise.

ANGELA: What?

MAXINE: I've got a bit of a surprise for you. Close your eyes.

ANGELA: Give over.

MAXINE: Come on, do as you're told. Close your eyes.

ANGELA: What for?

MAXINE: Just do it.

ANGELA: If this is sommat stupid I'll knack you. (*She closes her eyes.*)

MAXINE: Right now, no peeping.

ANGELA: Get on with it.

MAXINE: Just keep 'em closed. (*She exits. Off.*) Not yet. Not yet.

ANGELA: Hurry up.

MAXINE: (*Off.*) 'Ang on.

ANGELA: What you doin'?

MAXINE: (*She enters.*) 'Ang on. Right, you can open them.

ANGELA opens her eyes and standing in front of her is a spotty 24-year-old with long, lank hair. He is ungainly and doesn't appear to be very bright. He is dressed in scruffy denim and has patches of pop groups and Fred Flintstone badges stuck all over his clothes.

Well.

ANGELA: Well…

MAXINE: Meet the new member of our band.

ANGELA: Oh!

MAXINE: You don't seem very excited.

ANGELA: Oh dear, don't I?

MAXINE: Meet Monkey.

ANGELA: Monkey?

MAXINE: Monkey this is Angela, Angela this is Monkey.

MONKEY: (*Grunts.*) Alright.

ANGELA: Hello…Monkey. Maxine, can I have a little word please. (*She pulls MAXINE aside.*) What is that?

MAXINE: What?

They both look over their shoulders at MONKEY and smile at him. He looks at them vacantly.

ANGELA: Him! That! It! What the hell are you doing? Is this some kind of joke?

MAXINE: Hey, we were lucky to get him. There were a few bands after him.

ANGELA: It's not exactly Take That is it.

MAXINE: He's a good musician.

ANGELA: Maxine…he stinks.

MAXINE: Love Heart?

ANGELA: 'Dishy.'

MAXINE: 'Sexy legs.'

ANGELA: He's got to go.

MAXINE: Calm down. Calm down. You're flying off your head again over nowt.

ANGELA: What's he carrying?

MAXINE: They're his backing tapes, he's got hundreds. He's a professional.

MONKEY: Alright.

ANGELA: What's with the Flintstone badges?

MAXINE: Oh, that's his gimmick. He always wears them. He's renowned for 'em.

ANGELA: Listen you've just wheeled in Barny Rubble and you expect me to keep calm.

MAXINE: It's your moods again. Are you gonna give him a chance, for God's sake?

ANGELA: What's he doin'?

MAXINE: He's putting his demo tape on.

ANGELA: What?

MAXINE: Demo. Demonstration of his music. Don't you know owt?

ANGELA: Yeah.

MAXINE: This is him. This is his music. Take it away Monkey.

A huge guitar riff fills the room.

What more can I say?

ANGELA: Well, Monkey, that was pretty good. Welcome to the band. Can I get you anything to eat? Would you like a banana?

MAXINE: He knows loads of Madonna, don't you Monk?

MONKEY goes to the keyboard and plays the first few notes of 'Into the Groove' which is taken up by the P.A. and the music is used to bleed into the next scene.

Scene 6

ANGELA's bedroom. ANGELA is at the mirror preening her hair and singing and dancing to Madonna. VIV enters.

VIV: I bet you've just risen from the grave. (*She switches off the cassette.*)

ANGELA: I was listening to that.

VIV: I don't know what's come over you lately, you could sleep for England. You could have at least tidied up a bit. How can you live in this mess? (*She finds a parcel on the bed.*) What's this?

ANGELA: Oh, it's for you.

VIV: For me! Who from?

ANGELA: Me.

VIV: You.

ANGELA: Yeah. I saw it and…well, I thought that you might like it.

VIV: What is it?

ANGELA: Oh it's nowt. Open it and have a look.

VIV opens the parcel.

VIV: Angela.

ANGELA: What?

VIV: Ange, it's gorgeous. It's my colour. Hey, out of the way. (*She stands admiring herself in the mirror.*) You don't think it makes me look fat, do you?

ANGELA: Yeah. You look huge.

VIV: It must have cost a fortune. (*Pause.*) Hey, where do you get it?

ANGELA: I bought it.

VIV: What with?

ANGELA: Money. I bought it with money. Can you remember what that looks like?

VIV: Where did you get it from?

ANGELA: Oh this is bloody brilliant. I spend all my time saving up to buy you a present and this is the thanks I get, accused of pinching it.

VIV: I didn't say that.

ANGELA: What are you saying then?

VIV: It's brand new and…it's just that…what's it for…why?

ANGELA: Calm down, it's only a coat.

VIV: Thanks Angela. (*Pause.*) Right, that's it. I'm going to the hairdressers now. I hope Eileen can fit me in. I'm going out tonight now.

ANGELA: Since when have you needed an excuse to go out. You go out more often than the gas.

VIV: Sod off.

ANGELA: Well.

VIV: I won't be long.

VIV exits. Lights.

Scene 7

ANGELA's bedroom. ANGELA is looking out of the window waiting for MAXINE. MONKEY looks over her shoulder. ANGELA starts to wiggle her bum in time to Madonna's 'Cherish'. MONKEY notices this and sways his head in time with ANGELA's bum. ANGELA senses his presence, turns and sprays him with air freshener.

ANGELA: She shouldn't be long now, Monkey. I didn't know where the hell she's got to. I'll bloody kill her.

Enter MAXINE.

Where the hell 'ave you been?

MAXINE: Sorry, it was me dad. He shucked a bluey and it was difficult to get out of the house. Alright Monk.

ANGELA: We haven't got long and we need the practise.

MAXINE: I know, I'm sorry but you know what me dad's like when he loses his rag. Well, he got the phone bill this morning and you wanna see him. He's like a man possessed. And of course it was all my fault.

ANGELA: Well come on then, now you're here take you coat off and I'll get ready.

ANGELA exits. MAXINE self-consciously takes off her coat to reveal a ridiculous Madonna lookalike costume with large cones for her boobs. MONKEY laughs.

MAXINE: I'll chin you Monkey if you laugh at me. (*She sprays him.*)

ANGELA returns looking equally outrageous.

ANGELA: Nice, aren't they? Are you ready, Monkey? Have you got your words.

MAXINE: Well I know 'em sort of.

ANGELA: Do ya? Right, well I'm not too sure of the tune so you're gonna have to help us out.

MAXINE: Take it away, Monkey.

MONKEY is now wearing a ridiculous Viking helmet and the girls speak into microphones over the introduction to the song.

ANGELA: Ladies and gentlemen…

MAXINE: Live and direct from their sell-out world tour…

ANGELA: May I present to you…

MAXINE: The multi-million selling rock band…

ANGELA/MAXINE: Squashed Zits.

The girls embark on a heavy metal thrash of a song.

ANGELA:
BID WELCOME TO THE SISTERS OF SIN

MAXINE:
KNEEL BEFORE US AND THE PAIN WILL BEGIN

ANGELA:
I WILL BURN YOUR SOUL

MAXINE:
CAN YOU PAY THE TOLL?

MONKEY: (*Talking.*) It's a pound.

ANGELA/MAXINE:
> SEE US IN THE DARKNESS
> SNARLING EYES AND TEETH

ANGELA:
> WE'LL PUT YOU THROUGH THE MINCER

MAXINE:
> 'COS HUMANS TASTE LIKE BEEF

ANGELA/MAXINE:
> WE ARE VIKING TRAVELLERS
> LOST IN TIME AND SPACE

ANGELA:
> I WILL CHEW YOUR TESTICLES

MAXINE:
> I WILL BOIL YOUR FACE

ANGELA:
> I AM FANG THE WARRIORESS

MAXINE:
> I AM IRIS HELL

ANGELA/MAXINE:
> HE IS MAGIC MONKEY
> WHO CREATES AN EVIL SMELL

ANGELA:
> I AM QUEEN OF FIRE

MAXINE:
> I AM QUEEN OF RAIN

ANGELA/MAXINE:
> HE IS GOD OF PUNISHMENT
> AND YOU WILL FEEL THE PAIN

ANGELA:
> IF YOU BOW BEFORE US

MAXINE:

WE'LL GIVE YOU JUST ONE CHANCE

ANGELA/MAXINE:

THE ONLY WAY TO PLEASE US IS TO DRINK UP SATAN'S BLOOD
AND DANCE AND DANCE

ANGELA feels dizzy and, unnoticed by the others, she sits down.

MAXINE:

KNEEL BEFORE US, GAZE INTO OUT EYES
DO YOU KNOW THAT YOU'RE IN FOR A SURPRISE

The music equipment blows up propelling MONKEY through the air.

MONKEY: What happened? It's blown. Oh no, it's our kids.

MAXINE: Are you okay?

ANGELA: Yeah. I just came over all dizzy.

MAXINE: Monk, go and get her some water. Are you alright? Hurry up. What happened? Listen, Monkey can naff off from now on, we're singing songs about love and sex. Are you sure you're alright?

ANGELA: Yeah, I dunno what happened, I just came over all funny. I feel alright. I'm alright, honest. Just give us a minute.

MONKEY returns with a glass of water.

MAXINE: Well give her it then.

MONKEY hesitates and then chucks the water into her face.

Blackout.

Scene 8

*ANGELA's bedroom. ANGELA is in her bedroom. VIV enters wearing
a hat and coat. She is dressed up.*

VIV: Bloody showin' me up.

ANGELA: What you talkin' about?

VIV: You know.

ANGELA: What about you?

VIV: You know fine well what I'm talkin' about.

ANGELA: Have you seen yourself?

VIV: Talking to the doctor like that.

ANGELA: Wearing that bloody stupid hat.

VIV: I don't know where you think your manners are.

ANGELA: You look like you've just been to Ascot.

VIV: I didn't bring you up to talk like that. He was a doctor.

ANGELA: You don't say. Were you listening to him?

VIV: You think you're bloody clever, don't you?

ANGELA: Viv, we're gonna have to talk about this.

VIV: You can't talk about anything, there's no talking to
you. You're too busy trying to be bloody clever.

ANGELA: What about you? Why do you think I couldn't
tell you what was going on.

VIV: 'You're not very bright are you.' I was so bloody
embarrassed. He was only trying to help.

ANGELA: Help!

VIV: Yes, help, but you're too bloody smug to appreciate it.

ANGELA: I don't believe this.

VIV: It's knocking about with that Maxine.

ANGELA: 'Ere we go.

VIV: Wanting to be pop stars.

ANGELA: Viv.

VIV: Bloody Madonna.

ANGELA: Viv.

VIV: It'll be bloody drugs next.

ANGELA: For Christ's sake.

VIV: I'm not bloody stupid.

ANGELA: (*Shouting.*) Viv, stop it. Viv, will you bloody shut it for one minute. Were you listening to him?

Silence. They look at each other.

Do you know what he said? Were you listening to what he said? Viv, I've got Myeloid Leukemia. Do you know what that is? Viv, I've got cancer.

There is a long, long silence.

VIV: You're gonna have to help me a bit more round the house. You're bloody bone idle. I'm going out cleaning, I come back here and I have to start again. You're 16, you're gonna have to accept some more responsibility.

She stops and looks at ANGELA who hasn't moved, except for her eyes which have followed VIV round the room.

It's not too much to ask, is it? Is it? It's not too much to ask. I don't ask you for much when all's said and done.

She stops and looks at ANGELA again.

I was thinking about going on holiday, you and me.

ANGELA: Viv, stop it.

VIV: I've been thinking about it for a while now. This isn't a sudden thing.

ANGELA: Viv, don't.

VIV: Just you and me. You'd like that, wouldn't you. Blackpool, we could go to Blackpool.

ANGELA: Viv, will you stop it?

VIV: Or abroad. We could go abroad. Yes, that would be nice. Me and you.

ANGELA: Viv, we need to talk.

VIV: I'd like that. We'll get a bank loan. I've been thinking about this for a while now. A small bank loan. That'd be no problem. Spain. The sun. Laying on the beach. That's what we'll do. I've made up my mind.

ANGELA runs out.

There's no use arguing. You're gonna have to listen to me for a change. Spain'd be brilliant. (*She starts to sing.*) Viva España. Oh this year we're off to sunny Spain. Viva España.

She crumbles onto the bed in tears.

Lights and music.

End of Act One.

ACT TWO

Scene 1

Grangetown British Legion Club. MONKEY enters, walking round the stage with one arm raised aloft before making his way to his keyboard and amplifier. He has obviously been dressed by the girls with his waistcoat edged in blue fur. The girls then enter nervously a little bit in awe of the occasion. ANGELA is sporting a Madonna-type wig. They retrieve their microphones and adopt stylised positions upstage with their backs to the audience. We hear somebody blowing into a microphone and then banging it with his hand. We hear a voice-over.

VOICE: (*Off.*) Is it on Tommy? Can you hear me at the back of the room? Good. Right, ladies and gentlemen. Don't forget, your bingo books are on sale at the back of the concert room. Let's not leave it all until the last minute shall we. Right, now ladies and gentlemen, I'd like to move swiftly on because it's time for the first of tonight's cabaret artistes and tonight we've got a special treat. I'd like you to give a big Grangetown welcome for a local band who've just come back from a sell-out tour of Japan...

ANGELA breaks her pose and thumps MAXINE.

...and are making their first appearance here at the British Legion, so put your hands together and give a big British Legion welcome, ladies and gentlemen, for...Triangle.

MONKEY presses the backing tape and adopts a rock star pose. As the music starts and the lights come up, the girls move their bodies seductively as they improvise provocative groaning noises into the microphones. Eventually they leap round, the lights burst into full colour and they burst into song.

The girls embark upon a well-rehearsed – but ultimately tacky – dance routine. It is reminiscent of a bad pop video. As the song progresses MAXINE ignores the routine as she performs seductively to a member of the audience she fancies. ANGELA is furious.

ANGELA:
I'VE GOT RHYTHM

MAXINE:
AND I'VE GOT STYLE

ANGELA:
I'VE GOT THE LOVE

MAXINE:
AND I'VE GOT THE GUILE

ANGELA:
RESISTING IS FOOLISH

MAXINE:
YOU KNOW YOU CAN'T WIN

ANGELA/MAXINE:
SO LET'S MAKE MUSIC AND DICE WITH SIN

SO
COME TO ME
COME TO ME
I WANT YOU TO COME TO ME
COME TO ME
COME TO ME
COME TO ME
PARADISE IS HERE WITH ME
IF YOU WILL JUST COME TO ME.

ANGELA:
I'VE HAD SOME BOYS

MAXINE:
I'VE HAD SOME MEN

I'VE MADE LOVE WITH THE BEST OF THEM

ANGELA:

BUT NOW I'VE SET MY SIGHTS ON YOU

MAXINE:

I'VE GOT THE BODY AND YOU THE TATTOO

ANGELA/MAXINE:

SO
COME TO ME
COME TO ME
I WANT YOU TO COME TO ME
COME TO ME
COME TO ME
COME TO ME
PARADISE IS HERE WITH ME
IF YOU WILL JUST COME TO ME.

Dance sequence.

ANGELA:

I HAVE THE URGE AND THAT'S NOT ALL

MAXINE:

THIS PLAYING FIELD IS WAITING FOR YOUR BAT AND BALL

ANGELA:

I'M HOT AND STEAMY AND READY FOR YOU

ANGELA/MAXINE:

SO
COME TO ME
COME TO ME
I WANT YOU TO COME TO ME
COME TO ME
COME TO ME
COME TO ME
PARADISE IS HERE WITH ME
IF YOU WILL JUST COME TO ME.

MAXINE: Good evening, Grangetown. Are yas havin' a good night? He looks nice in the front row. Whoops, just a minute, I've got me knickers stuck up me bum. I hate that, don't you, when you get a wedgy. It's these new outfits. Do you like them? Cheeky, aren't they?

ANGELA grabs MAXINE and pulls her upstage.

ANGELA: What the hell are you doin'?

MAXINE: Ow gerroff.

ANGELA: What do you think you're playing at?

MAXINE: I'm just 'avin' a bit of patter with the audience.

ANGELA: Well it's shite.

MAXINE: They like it.

ANGELA: It's embarrassing.

MAXINE: Who do you think you are, like?

ANGELA: I'm not bloody cheap and embarrassing.

MAXINE: I'm gonna chin you in a minute.

ANGELA: We look like battered Battenburg cakes.

MAXINE: What about that bloody hairpiece of yours? You never have it off. You bloody hypocrite. You look like a bloody Barbie doll. And I want me money back.

ANGELA: Don't worry about that. You'll get your pigging money back. I don't break promises or lie.

MAXINE: And I suppose I do. Why don't you get a friggin' bath you stink?

ANGELA: You're not bothered who you upset.

MAXINE: I couldn't give a monkeys. So I'm a liar now am I?

ANGELA: You'd say owt to get into someone's trousers. The way you carry on in Madison, it's disgusting, throwing yourself at everything that shows the slightest bit of interest. You're cheap.

MAXINE: Oh yeah. What about you and Graeme Finchley?

ANGELA: Don't you dare say owt about him, that was different.

MAXINE: Was it?

ANGELA: Yes!

MAXINE: Was it?

ANGELA: You know it was different. We were going out with each other.

MAXINE: You only went out twice.

ANGELA: I thought he loved me.

MAXINE: Oh don't give me that shit.

ANGELA: What about the night you shagged Darren Beech in the bloody Madison car park?

MAXINE: I did not.

ANGELA: Yes you did 'cos Marie told me.

MAXINE: Was she there, like?

ANGELA: I wouldn't be surprised if half of Madison was there.

MAXINE: Right, that does it, you can stick your band right up your arse.

ANGELA: Good. Now maybe we'll get somewhere, won't we, Monkey?

MAXINE: I wouldn't bet on it. (*MAXINE storms to the exit, stops and turns.*) Fuck off and die.

ANGELA breaks down and cuddles MONKEY. She realises he stinks and breaks away and exits. MONKEY is left alone on stage. He looks decidedly uncomfortable. He grins at the audience. He makes his way to his keyboard and attempts to play 'The Flintstones' theme tune which goes well until he hits a final bum note gets embarrassed and exits.

Scene 2

The Leyton living room. VIV hovers near the door. As soon as she hears a noise she quickly sits on the settee and pretends to do a crossword. ANGELA enters wearing the same Madonna wig and a huge Madonna T-shirt. She flops on the settee next to VIV. Silence. VIV casts surreptitious glances as ANGELA plucks up the courage to speak.

ANGELA: What's me dad like?

VIV: Two arms, two legs, the body of big daddy and the brains of Kermit the Frog. What do you mean what's he like?

ANGELA: I mean…you know…what's he like?

VIV: He's like a bad smell.

ANGELA: Viv, come on.

VIV: What you on about?

ANGELA: I'm just curious.

VIV: What's brought this on?

ANGELA: Nowt. I just wondered what he was like.

Pause.

VIV: What's brought this on all of a sudden?

ANGELA: Forget it.

VIV: What's up?

ANGELA: Doesn't matter.

VIV: Come on.

ANGELA: It doesn't matter.

VIV: I know something's up so you might as well tell me.

ANGELA: I was just thinking about him. I just wondered what he was like.

Silence.

VIV: 'E was alright. A right one of the lads, or at least he thought he was. (*She smiles.*) Despite everything…despite everything…I well…he was alright.

ANGELA: But you said…

VIV: I know I've said a lot of things and I'll never forgive him for what he's done to me… and you. He did some bloody funny things. I'll never forget the first time I took him, or should I say dragged him, shopping. He kept disappearing, and then I found him stood on Linthorpe Road with about ten other blokes, staring into Curry's window. I thought there must have been a sale on or somebody had collapsed in the window or sommat like that, but there they were, glued to the teleprinter, waiting for the bloody football results. He was popular. He was always the life and soul of any company we were in.

ANGELA: Do you miss him?

VIV: No!

Silence.

ANGELA: Are you alright, Viv?

VIV: Have you had any breakfast? You want to get something to eat.

ANGELA: I know, there's people all over the world would be glad of this food.

VIV: I just want you to…

ANGELA: Alright, I'm gonna get sommat.

VIV: What time did you come in this morning?

ANGELA: I dunno.

VIV: I was awake until half past three.

ANGELA: I'll get some cornflakes.

VIV: We've got some Variety Pack.

ANGELA: Eh?

VIV: Were you out with Maxine?

ANGELA: Variety Pack. You never buy Variety Pack.

VIV: Eh? Oh! Err, there was a special offer on.

ANGELA: I thought they were too expensive.

VIV: You know, they were in one of those baskets with lots of things on special offer.

ANGELA: I thought we couldn't afford them.

VIV: Well I dunno, they must be damaged or somebody must have made a mistake.

ANGELA: Forget it, I'll do without.

VIV: But you've got to have something to eat. You've got to keep your strength up.

ANGELA: No, it doesn't matter. The milk's been left out anyway and I hate warm milk on my cereal.

VIV: I've had a terrible night's sleep. Do you want some toast?

ANGELA: Yeah, go on then.

VIV: So it was a good night.

ANGELA: It was alright.

VIV: Where did you go?

ANGELA: Madison.

VIV: 'Til quarter to six.

Silence.

ANGELA: I'm off down town after me breakfast, gonna do a bit of shopping. Do you want owt?

VIV: Where were you until quarter to six?

ANGELA: For crying out loud, will you give it a rest.

VIV: I'm just concerned, I worry about you.

ANGELA: Mother, you are smothering me. I don't need Variety Pack. Weetabix will do. We've always had Weetabix or cornflakes and now all of a sudden you're buying Variety Pack. I don't need it. It's too expensive! Viv, I know that you care and you're only doing this for me but I don't need it. I'm alright. I'm okay. Honest.

Lights and music.

Scene 3

ANGELA's bedroom. ANGELA is laid on her bed listening to Madonna, reading a magazine and eating an orange. The door tentatively opens and MAXINE apprehensively enters. As the door clicks shut ANGELA realises MAXINE is there and switches off the cassette. The atmosphere is very brittle.

MAXINE: Alright.

ANGELA: Alright.

MAXINE: Yeah.

Pause.

Listen I'm sorry for what I said.

ANGELA: So am I.

MAXINE instantly relaxes and the tension disappears.

MAXINE: I was dreading coming round.

ANGELA: Let's just forget it.

MAXINE: Ya should know what I'm like with my big mouth, always shoutin' it off. Hey, I think your hair's smashing. I think I might get one. Hey, I saw your mam in Lanny's, she said that you weren't that well.

ANGELA: Her mouth's bigger than yours.

MAXINE: Hey, let's not push it. Hey, how do you fancy going to see the Chippendales? They're getting a trip up from the Stap. They're on at the City Hall, Newcastle.

ANGELA: Yeah, when is it?

MAXINE: A week on Friday. The bus leaves at quarter past six from the Stap so if we get there early we'll be able to sink a few before we get on the bus.

ANGELA: Shit, that's the twenty-fourth.

MAXINE: So.

ANGELA: I can't go. Shit!

MAXINE: What?

ANGELA: I can't. I'd love to but I can't.

MAXINE: Not again. It was the same last month. What's the excuse this time?

ANGELA: There's no excuse. I've got something on.

MAXINE: What?

ANGELA: Look I can't make it. I'd love to but I can't.

MAXINE: You're going funny. I don't know what you're being so secretive for all of a sudden. There's sommat funny going on.

ANGELA: I'm sure it wasn't the same last month.

MAXINE: Yes it was. You wouldn't come and see Chubby Brown 'cos you claimed you had a date with a bloke nobody had heard of and you missed an absolutely brilliant night. There must have been five thousand people all shouting you fat bastard, you fat bastard.

ANGELA: Well, that wasn't my fault. You can't blame me for that. They were probably drunk.

Pause. MAXINE glares at ANGELA in disbelief.

MAXINE: Not at me you stupid piece of afterbirth, at Chubby. He was brilliant, 'I'm no gynaecologist but I'll have a bloody good look at it for you.' It was a scream. Come on. Last time I laughed so much I wet myself. They're brilliant. They're dead erotic.

ANGELA: I can't.

MAXINE: (*Sings.*) 'Erotic, erotic put your hands all over my body.'

ANGELA: Gerroff. Listen I've got something to tell you – and show you.

MAXINE: Hey, you're not a lezzy are ya?

ANGELA: Maxine!

MAXINE: Thank Christ for that, but you never know these days. Sometimes I think I'm not normal 'cos I fancy the arse off Jamie Power.

ANGELA meanwhile has removed her Madonna wig to reveal that she is almost bald except for clumps of long, thin whispy hair. MAXINE is initially stunned.

MAXINE: You can get lost.

ANGELA: What?

MAXINE: No. That's pathetic. I'm not gettin' me hair cut like that for anybody. A gimmick is one thing but that's ridiculous. Hey, it looks bloody stupid. You look pig-ugly. Who cut it? I'll get 'em for you. It's one thing 'avin' a sense of humour but that's bloody ridiculous.

ANGELA: I'm ill.

MAXINE: Well you don't look very well that's for sure.

ANGELA: No, listen motormouth, I'm poorly, that's why I'm like this. I'm ill.

MAXINE: Shit!

Silence.

Shit.

MAXINE walks round ANGELA studying her head.

Shit.

ANGELA: What do you keep saying that for?

MAXINE: I dunno what else to say. (*Pause.*) Shit. It's not the measles then.

They look at each other for a while and then start to laugh.

ANGELA: Why can't you take owt seriously?

MAXINE: I do, it's just I dunno what to say. You know how I feel don't ya.

ANGELA: Yeah.

MAXINE: Listen if there's owt I can do you've just…

ANGELA: Yeah.

MAXINE: You could start selling Tefal pans.

ANGELA: Piss off.

MAXINE: Sorry.

Pause.

'Phone home.' (*She laughs.*) I can't help it. So that's why you've been wearing that hairpiece. It all fits in now. Actually it doesn't look that bad. I quite like it.

ANGELA: Piss off.

MAXINE: No, you look quite nice.

ANGELA: Shite.

MAXINE: How long before it starts growing back again?

ANGELA: It's not, Maxine. It's not gonna grow back. This is it. This is goodnight, God bless.

A long silence.

MAXINE: You mean it's…

ANGELA: Yeah. It's a bummer, isn't it?

MAXINE: Shit!

ANGELA: Don't start that again.

MAXINE: Why didn't you tell me?

ANGELA: I couldn't. It took me long enough to tell myself. And when I started this chemo lark…

MAXINE: This what?

ANGELA: Chemo. Chemotherapy. They said when I started it there might be some side effects. They said if you lose your hair, you'll get it back, but I saw the doctor the other day. Well, it's not working. They were hoping for some remission but, well, there you go.

MAXINE: So what are you saying?

ANGELA: For God's sake, Maxine, shall I draw you a picture?

MAXINE: Have you told Viv?

ANGELA: Yeah.

MAXINE: Why don't you sort yourself out? You never do anything normal. Just when we were getting the group going.

ANGELA: Well I'm not exactly chuffed about it.

Silence. They cuddle.

Music and lights.

Scene 4

ANGELA's bedroom. MAXINE enters wearing sunglasses, posing and singing.

MAXINE: It's happened.

ANGELA: What has?

MAXINE: What every girl in Middlesbrough dreams about.

ANGELA: You mean…

MAXINE: Yeah.

They embrace and scream.

ANGELA: When…when?

MAXINE: He phoned me.

ANGELA: He didn't.

MAXINE: He did.

ANGELA: Who did?

MAXINE: You what?

ANGELA: Who phoned you?

MAXINE: Jamie Power, ya gowk.

ANGELA: You're joking.

MAXINE: No.

ANGELA: He phoned ya.

MAXINE: Yeah.

ANGELA: After all this time, Jamie Power decides to phone you.

MAXINE: Eh?

ANGELA: After all the beauty queens he's been out with, he now phones you.

MAXINE: You what!

ANGELA: He now resorts to phoning up Maxine.

MAXINE: I'll bloody crack you one in a minute.

ANGELA: Eh? Oh no sorry, I didn't mean it like that. It's just that he's been out with some real stunners. I mean he went out with Alexandra Hamilton and she's a model.

MAXINE: And what's the matter with me, like. I suppose I look like a bulldog chewing a toffee.

ANGELA: No Max, I didn't mean it like that. He's lucky to get you. In fact you're too good for him. You are. You're natural. You've got a personality.

MAXINE: I've got a face a dog wouldn't lick but a lovely personality.

ANGELA: No, you're good fun. Good to be with. Not like all those plastic tarts who think they're sommat. I bet they all shag on the first date. I mean you wouldn't do anything as cheap and common as that.

MAXINE looks knowingly at ANGELA.

Maxine, you never. Maxine, you didn't.

MAXINE nods. They both scream.

When?

MAXINE: Well, he phoned me this morning. I nearly wet meself when I realised it was him. I played it dead cool. I was as charismatic as shit.

ANGELA: Oway then what happened?

MAXINE: We called round his house to pick up his football kit 'cos he was going training and there was no one in. His mam and dad were out and, well, there you are, it happened. It was fab – u – lous.

ANGELA: I hope you took precautions.

MAXINE: Course we did. Do you think I'm stupid? We locked both doors and put the bolts in.

ANGELA: I mean did you…

MAXINE: I know what you mean and we did. He was so manly and…and…rough.

ANGELA: Was it brilliant?

Pause as MAXINE looks at ANGELA.

MAXINE: (*Cool.*) It was alright. Ya know…not bad. I've had better. It was fantastic.

ANGELA: What was the difficulty rating?

MAXINE: Difficulty rating about one and a half, ecstasy rating ten million.

ANGELA: How big was it?

MAXINE: You what?

ANGELA: You heard. Come on, how big was it?

MAXINE: Angela! (*Pause.*) It was about…let's see it must have been…this big.

They laugh.

It looked like one of me dad's burnt barbecued sausages. I could 'ave stirred me cup of tea with it. After it was all over his cute little tail went all wrinkly and floppy.

ANGELA: His cute little what?

MAXINE: Tail. That's what our Darren calls it. What's wrong with that?

ANGELA: You don't call it 'tail.'

MAXINE: Course you do. That's what we call it in our house. What do you call it then?

ANGELA: Cock.

MAXINE starts to take off her tights. They are badly torn.

MAXINE: Honestly, Angela, you're dead common sometimes. You are. You shock me. Common as muck. Can you lend us a pair of tights 'cos these have exploded.

ANGELA: Look at the bloody state of them.

MAXINE: It's passion. He was like an animal. It's what I do to people. It's just the way…

ANGELA throws her some clean tights.

ANGELA: Here.

MAXINE: Ta. Men are when they're with me. Uncontrollable. Right, oway.

ANGELA: Where are we going?

MAXINE: The pub.

ANGELA: You what.

MAXINE: I need a drink after that cheeky little rush of excitement. It's got my juices flowing.

ANGELA: Look at the state of me. I look a mess.

MAXINE: Just throw a bit of slap on and we'll nip down for the last half-hour.

ANGELA: No, you go. I don't feel up to it.

MAXINE: It's just for a couple. It's just for the last half-hour. Come on we'll have a laugh like we used to.

ANGELA: Maybe tomorrow.

MAXINE: You're always saying things like that. Come on, there's a karaoke on. I'll do my Shirley Bassey impressions. 'As long as he needs me…'

ANGELA: I'd love to but I…

MAXINE: But nothing. Come on, the night is young and so am I. I've got new batteries in my ghetto blaster and I'm ready to pump up the volume, so grab your coat and let's hit the pub. What do you say?

ANGELA: I don't want to.

MAXINE: For God's sake, stop feeling sorry for yourself.

Pause.

ANGELA: Look, just go.

Pause.

MAXINE: I know it's difficult but you've got t̲
most of it. You've got to try and live a bit.

ANGELA: I've got to live a bit. Maxine, I'm dying,
know why but I am. I don't know why I've been p
to have such a shit-awful life. What have I done tha̲ s so
bloody wrong? So you can piss off with your, 'Let's be
jolly,' routine. With your 'Let's pretend everything's
alright and we'll have a laugh like we used to in the
old days.'

MAXINE: I just thought…

ANGELA: You just thought. That's your bloody problem,
you don't think. You put that mouth of yours into mega-
drive and off you go. I'm dying and I wish I wasn't. I
wish it wasn't me. I wish it was you. That's shocked you,
hasn't it? You're gonna die. Oh yeah, everybody's gonna
die. But the difference is I'm gonna die a lot sooner. Why
aren't I normal? Why does nothing normal ever happen
to me? I've not got a dad. You are so lucky and you don't
know it…And you're so bloody insensitive, always going
on about our dad this and our dad that… I'm sick of you
going on about your shitting dad. Mine can't even be
bothered to come and see me. I'd give anything to have
a normal dad who'd talk to me and give me a cuddle…
and comfort me. Is that too much to ask? A normal life.
Is that too much to ask? Do you know something?
(*Pause.*) I've never had sex. I'm a virgin. Yeah I know
what I said, what we said, but…well, they were just
stories full of me, us trying to be grown-up. But I'm not
gonna grow up. I'll never grow up and be a woman and
have children. Why me? Why the fucking hell does it
have to be me? It's not fair. How would you feel if
someone told you that you were gonna die? Come on,
it's not easy is it? YOU ARE GOING TO DIE. You have
got four weeks to live. What are you going to do?
(*Pause.*) It's not easy, is it, and people are so full of
understanding… so full of shit. 'I'd go on holiday, I'd

travel.' What is the point in spending your time in strange lands with strange people? So you'll have lots of happy memories and photographs to look back on. When? I haven't got time, I'm dying. What's the point in laying on a beach getting a tan? So I'll look good in my coffin. So people will be able to gork into my coffin with…with… tear-stained eyes and say…'She looks really good'…'She's the best suntanned corpse I've ever seen'…Well, they can all fuck off. Sometimes I feel as though I should have dignity and write poems and raise money for charity an' all that… Be a symbol for other people to look up to. But why should I? What has anybody ever done for me? Look at you, you're pathetic stood there not wanting to say anything in case you hurt my feelings. Making excuses for me. 'It's her condition… It's understandable…She's just a bit down.' Well don't patronise me. Tell me to fuck off. Slap me. Go on. (*She pushes MAXINE.*) Go on. (*She pushes her again.*) Go on, do something.

MAXINE: Listen I'll come back…

ANGELA: You haven't got the guts. You're gutless. You're a coward. Look at you. Well, maybe if I carried on like you, dying wouldn't be such a bad thing.

MAXINE: Angela, why are you saying this? I'm going.

ANGELA: Go on, you slut…Go on with your childish dreaming…'I wanna be on "Top of the Pops", I wanna be on "This is Your Life"'. Your life, your life! Go on, piss off.

MAXINE grabs her coat, bag and shoes and runs to the door. ANGELA shoves her as she goes.

I don't wanna see you again, you tramp. Go on tramp, trollop, slut, bag, piss off, piss off, piss off, piss off.

ANGELA beats on the door. Silence. Slowly ANGELA turns walks and picks up Oscar. Madonna singing 'Cherish' plays over the P.A. VIV enters and starts to strip ANGELA's bedroom. After a while she is joined by MAXINE who helps her. The bedroom is transformed into a hospital bedroom. It is clinical and bare.

Scene 5

A hospital bedroom. KEN enters tentatively.

KEN: Angela?

Silence.

ANGELA: Bloody hell.

Pause.

KEN: Alright.

Silence.

ANGELA: What's the matter, your conscience getting the better of you?

KEN: I just wanted to…you know…see how you… to have a chat type of thing.

ANGELA: Don't think you're doing this for me 'cos you're not. You're doing it for *you* so you can ease your own mind, your own conscience.

KEN: Look perhaps I'd better go. Maybe this wasn't a good idea.

Silence.

You've changed.

ANGELA: Don't tell me: 'By hell you haven't half grown.'

Pause.

KEN: Can I get you anything?

ANGELA: Ten Embassy wouldn't go amiss.

KEN: What?

ANGELA: Keep your hair on, I'm only joking.

KEN: How's Viv?

ANGELA: Brilliant. (*Pause.*) Why have you never been to see me?

KEN: I don't know. It wasn't…It's not easy.

ANGELA: I think we've established that things aren't easy, but that doesn't alter things. I used to cry myself to sleep, praying to God that you'd come back and everything would get back to normal, and then when I realised that you were never coming back, I prayed that you'd come and see me.

KEN: I wanted to, believe me I wanted to but I had to make a complete break, I felt it was best just to stay away, let everybody start again.

ANGELA: What about me?

KEN: Don't think I haven't thought about you.

ANGELA: Oh that makes me feel great. You thought about me.

KEN: If I'd kept coming back to see you, I'd've just kept…well…I don't know…I suppose I thought it'd just make things worse.

ANGELA: You couldn't've made it any worse. (*Pause.*) I heard you got married again.

KEN: Yeah.

ANGELA: Any children?

KEN: I don't think talking about me is gonna do any good. That's not why I'm here.

ANGELA: Why are you here?

KEN: I dunno. I...I...I wanted to see you.

ANGELA: Look I need to know. Have you got any kids?

KEN: Yeah. Two girls, satisfied.

ANGELA: What do you call them?

KEN: Angela, this is pointless.

ANGELA: What do you call them?

KEN: Charlotte and Louise.

ANGELA: Oh.

Silence.

I'm glad that you came. Thanks, but Viv's due back any minute and I think it's probably best that she doesn't know that you've been.

KEN: Yeah. Look if there's anything I can get you, or do for you, you've just got to ask.

ANGELA: No thanks. We've managed to survive without you so far, I don't want anything from you.

KEN: Well if you change your mind you've just got to ask. I'd do anything.

ANGELA: Did you say anything?

KEN: Yeah.

ANGELA: Right, well there is one thing that you could do for me. I've never asked you for anything before. Are you sure? I mean I don't know you.

KEN: I know it looks bad and you've got all sorts of reasons for hating me…and I know nothing I can do can make amends for what's happened… but…well…you are still…well my…if there's anything I can do just give me the chance and I promise I'll try.

ANGELA: You promise.

KEN: I promise. Honest, you've got my word on it.

ANGELA: Well I'm really worried about Viv. I want you to look after her…make sure she's alright… help her…be there for her.

Silence.

KEN: That's not gonna be easy…I mean I've got a family… A wife and kids.

ANGELA: You promised, you gave your word but maybe that was expecting too much of you. I mean you gave a promise once before in the eyes of God and you soon broke that.

KEN: I just don't know how. Anything else, anything but that.

ANGELA: You know what I keep thinking about. I know it sounds stupid but…well…I just keep thinking about where she's gonna have her Christmas dinner. Why is it so important where people have their Christmas dinner? I just picture her sat there alone. I don't want her to be alone.

Pause.

KEN: Okay. Alright. I'll try. I will. I'll do my best.

ANGELA: Promise me.

KEN: I promise.

ANGELA: Look, she'll be here any second so it's perhaps best she doesn't see you just yet.

KEN: Yeah, right I'll get going then.

KEN moves as if to go and cuddle ANGELA. She braces herself to receive him, but he pauses for a long while before turning and exiting. ANGELA breaks down.

ANGELA: Well Oscar, do you believe him? No, I can't make my mind up either but we'll see.

VIV enters in a hurry. ANGELA turns away and grabs a tissue to clean her face.

VIV: I've just popped in. I'm not staying I've just brought you some clean things.

ANGELA: You've got a big mouth.

VIV: What?

ANGELA: You've been round to Maxine's, haven't you?

VIV: Come again.

ANGELA: You've been round to Maxine's, haven't you?

Pause.

VIV: Yeah. Yes, I have. Well I had to. This is stupid. Somebody had to say something. For God's sake, you and Maxine have been friends for such a long time. I just tried to make things normal again, if you know what I mean. How do you know?

ANGELA: She's been in this afternoon.

VIV: Oh.

ANGELA: It was nice to see her. We had a laugh. She's the craziest person I know. (*Pause.*) Thanks Viv.

VIV: I'll change your water.

ANGELA: You change the water every time you come in. I think you're becoming obsessed with clean water.

VIV: Well it's horrible drinking warm water, you know it is. I've brought you some magazines.

ANGELA: Listen, you haven't forgotten about the Madonna songs, have you?

VIV: For the hundredth time, no. 'Like a Virgin', 'Holiday' and 'Cherish'. I've had it all cleared. Everything'll be just as you want it.

ANGELA: Hey, you're late. That's not like you.

VIV: No, I've just been to the estate agents. I've never said anything before but…I'm thinking of selling the house.

ANGELA: What for? We've had some great times in that house.

VIV: Yeah that's it. That's why.

ANGELA: You don't wanna go doin' owt rash. Give yourself a bit of time to sort things out. Just hang fire for a little while.

VIV: No, this hasn't happened all of a sudden. I've been thinking about it for a while. It's not gonna be easy but I've made up my mind. We've had some cracking times in that house, you and me.

ANGELA: Can you remember the time we played hide and seek…I think I must have been about four or five and you couldn't find me.

VIV: How could I forget. I ended up running up and down the street demented, asking all the kids in the street and the neighbours if they'd seen you.

ANGELA: An' I'd climbed into the washing machine and fallen asleep.

VIV: You've always been a bloody nuisance. Anyway I've made up my mind, I'm gonna sell it.

ANGELA: You'll end up in naughty Nunthorpe going to coffee mornings and walking your Chihuahua to the shops for some herbal tea.

VIV: Sod off.

ANGELA: Are you sure?

VIV: Yeah.

ANGELA: Well you make sure my house goes to a good home.

VIV: Oh hey, I heard from those families.

ANGELA: I meant to ask you about that.

VIV: Yeah, it looks as though they're gonna take me on so I'll be almost full-time.

ANGELA: Brilliant.

VIV: Yeah, it's washing out me cloths that gets them. Is that the time? I don't believe it. I don't know where the day's gone. Listen, I'm sorry angel, but I'm gonna have to make a move.

ANGELA: Don't worry, I'll see you tomorrow.

VIV: Right, I'll see you later. Oh I've got you some chocolates with your magazines.

ANGELA: Look, go or you'll be late.

VIV leans over and kisses ANGELA.

See you.

VIV: Tarra.

ANGELA: Good luck.

VIV exits. ANGELA looks in the bag. She finds 20 Embassy and a box of matches. She is surprised. She looks after VIV. She smiles.

Lights and music.

Scene 6

A hospital bedroom. ANGELA is sitting on the bed. Her situation has deteriorated somewhat. MAXINE bursts into the room.

MAXINE: Sorry I'm late. What a bloody day. I feel as though I've got me head up my arse. I missed the bus, the next one didn't turn up and our Darren came home from school last night with two white mice in a cage that he'd bought. Well, he got up this morning, the cage was there but the mice weren't. You can imagine the state of our house. It's been turned upside down looking for Gigsy and Cantona but can we hell find 'em. Me mam's gone off her head, our dad's gone to the club and our Darren's been banished to his room and grounded for the rest of his life. Right, so how are you? You look like shit.

ANGELA: Thanks.

MAXINE: Welcome. Oh here, I've got you a little something.

ANGELA: What is it?

MAXINE: Well open it.

ANGELA: It's a travel bag.

MAXINE: Yeah.

ANGELA: Where the hell do you think I'm going? Maybe I'll just take it up to the pearly gates, I'm sure it'll go well in heaven.

MAXINE: You're countin' your chickens a bit, aren't you?

ANGELA: Ya cheeky cow.

MAXINE: It's got a picture of Madonna on it.

ANGELA: While we're dishing out presents, I've got something for you.

MAXINE: (*Sending it up.*) Oh for me. What's this?

ANGELA: What does it look like?

MAXINE: I know it's money, I'm not stupid but I don't want your money.

ANGELA: It's the money I owe you for me mam's coat.

Silence.

MAXINE: I don't want this.

ANGELA: Well you made enough song and dance about it when you lent us it. Besides, I'm not 'avin' you calling me when I'm gone.

MAXINE: You're not a full box. Well, I'll be able to go out tonight now.

ANGELA: Thanks a lot.

MONKEY enters.

Hello, bloody hell. What are you doin' here?

MAXINE: Who let you out on a Thursday?

MONKEY: Alright.

ANGELA: (*Imitating him.*) Alright.

MAXINE: Alright.

Pause.

MONKEY: Alright.

MAXINE: You're a hell of a conversationalist, Monk.

ANGELA: I bet those long November nights fly past in your house.

MONKEY hands ANGELA a small paper bag.

MONKEY: Here.

MAXINE: He speaks. It speaks.

ANGELA: For me. What is it?

MAXINE: You do say some bloody stupid things. It's like bloody Christmas with all these presents. Hurry up, it might be Milk Tray and I love Milk Tray.

ANGELA: It's a bag of salted peanuts.

MAXINE: Romance has never been your strong point, has it, Monk? You're supposed to bring chocolates or grapes or lucozade or…

ANGELA: Shut up Max, it's the thought. Thanks Monkey.

MAXINE: Well give her a kiss then.

MONKEY looks horrified and ANGELA glares at MAXINE.

Go on Monk. Shot the lips on her.

ANGELA: Don't embarrass him.

MAXINE: (*Shouts an order.*) Monkey!

MONKEY leans over and kisses ANGELA.

There ya go, it's nice, isn't it, Monk?

ANGELA: Thanks for the nuts, Monkey.

MONKEY: Oh errr…here…

MAXINE: What is it?

ANGELA: It's a couple of packets of Love Hearts. Oh Monkey, you soft sod.

MAXINE: Hey, where's mine?

MONKEY: Right…errrr…Alright. (*He exits.*)

MAXINE: He's a bugger. (*Pause.*) Ange, are you scared?

ANGELA: I'm shitting it.

MAXINE: I would be. (*Pause.*) What do you think you'll miss the most?

ANGELA slowly turns and glares at MAXINE in disgust.

ANGELA: I thought you'd come to cheer me up, ya morbid bugger.

MAXINE: Sorry.

Pause.

I'd miss a Woolworth's Pic 'n Mix. And Diamond White. And Torville and Dean. If he's not giving her one, I've not got a hole in my arse. I cried when they got that bronze medal. So did me dad.

Pause. She looks at ANGELA who smiles at her.

He wouldn't admit it but he did an awful lot of blowing his nose.

ANGELA: I'll miss Oscar.

Pause.

MAXINE: I like a good shit.

ANGELA: I've never known anyone stink like you.

MAXINE: Listen to Chanel arse.

MAXINE: I want you to do me a favour.

MAXINE: Name it, it's done.

ANGELA: I don't want you to come and see me any more.

Pause.

MAXINE: Listen, don't be daft, I don't mind, I enjoy comin' to see you. Mates and all that.

ANGELA: I'd rather you didn't.

MAXINE: Don't be stupid. You're my best friend. I've never had a friend like you. I want to come.

ANGELA: Don't make this difficult for me. Maxine, I don't want you to come. I don't want you to come.

Silence.

MAXINE: But I…

ANGELA: Promise me.

Silence. MAXINE is overcome but she fights it.

MAXINE: Yeah. (*Silence.*) Listen if there's owt I can do for you or if you change your mind, you've just got to say.

ANGELA: Hey, there is sommat.

MAXINE: What?

ANGELA: Well, Jill who looks after me has been brilliant.

MAXINE: Yeah I know.

ANGELA: Well, she said she goes in Harvey's nearly every Saturday. So if you see her in there, do us a favour and buy her a Diamond White from me.

MAXINE: Shite do you know how much Diamond Whites cost in there?

ANGELA: You tight get.

MAXINE: Well I'm saving up for me holidays.

Pause.

Hey I nearly forgot, we've got a gig at the Mall on Saturday night.

ANGELA: The Mall.

MAXINE: Yeah.

ANGELA: That's brilliant.

MAXINE: It's official an' all. It was in the Gazette.

ANGELA: Bloody hell.

MAXINE: Me mam cut it out. She's got it stuck on the fridge behind the magnetic rabbit.

ANGELA: What's she like, I wouldn't dare.

MAXINE: Yeah but the most exciting thing is that we've got a load of agents from record companies coming to see us. We sent out loads of demo tapes and we've got loads of interest.

ANGELA: If you make it on 'Top of the Pops' without me, I'll come back as a bloody ghost and haunt you.

MAXINE: It's just my voice they've fell in love with.

ANGELA: How many's definitely comin'?

MAXINE: Oh let's see there must be five or six.

ANGELA: Maxine!

MAXINE: None. But I was talking to this bloke in Harvey's last week who said he knew a record producer and he was gonna try and get him to come.

ANGELA: You're bloody terrible, you.

MAXINE: Hey, he was alright an' all, he got me drinks in all night.

ANGELA: As long as that's all he got.

VIV enters. MAXINE turns away. She is upset.

VIV: Err…right…look, I've forgotten your water. I'll just nip to the kiosk and buy you a bottle. (*She exits.*)

MAXINE: Well look, I'll get going.

ANGELA: Right.

MAXINE: Bye Angela

ANGELA: Yeah. Hey.

MAXINE: What?

ANGELA: Love Heart.

MAXINE: 'Sexy supermodel with a gorgeous body.'

ANGELA: 'Big Boy.'

MAXINE: I wish. (*She walks to the door.*)

ANGELA: Maxine.

    MAXINE stops, but doesn't turn around.

    Alright.

MAXINE: Alright. (*She exits.*)

    Silence.

    VIV enters.

VIV: Do you need anything? Would you like a drink or anything?

ANGELA: No, it's alright. (*Pause.*) Did you go out last night?

VIV: Just for that last hour. Went up the Stap. Bit quiet really. Oh, Margaret Sigsworth was asking after you.

ANGELA: Viv, will you give all my Madonna tapes to Maxine, that's if you don't want them.

VIV: Yeah. Well, I might keep a couple.

ANGELA: Listen Viv, would you mind if I skipped today's visit?

VIV: What do you mean?

ANGELA: I feel a bit tired and I think I'll have to have a little nap.

VIV: Are you alright? Would you like me to get the nurse? I'll just...

ANGELA: No, I'm alright. I just feel a bit tired.

VIV: Are you sure there's nowt I can get you?

ANGELA: No, honest. I'm okay. I just feel a bit bad about dragging you all this way.

VIV: Don't be stupid, it doesn't bother me. As long as you're okay. Are you sure there's nowt I can get you?

ANGELA: Yeah I'm fine.

VIV: I'll get going then, leave you to get some rest.

VIV kisses ANGELA and walks to the door.

ANGELA: Mam.

VIV stops dead. Slowly she turns round. ANGELA holds out her teddy bear.

Will you look after Oscar for me?

Silence.

VIV: Yeah. Goodnight God bless.

ANGELA: Goodnight God bless.

VIV turns and exits quickly.

ANGELA is alone on the bed. She draws her knees up to herself and thinks. We hear Madonna singing 'Like a Prayer'. The lights slowly fade to black.

The End.